PRE-READING

CHRISTMAS

A FIRST BOOK FOR PIANO

Written and Arranged by Nancy and Randall Faber

Production: Frank and Gail Hackinson

Production Coordinator: Marilyn Cole

Book Design: Gwen Terpstra Design, San Francisco

Christmas Story Illustrations: Lori Andrus

Music Editors: Edwin McLean and Victoria McArthur

Engraving: Music Craft of Hollywood, Inc. (Fla.)
Terry Harr

FABER
PIANO ADVENTURES
3042 Creek Drive
Ann Arbor, Michigan 48108

A Note to Teachers

This Christmas introduce your pre-reading students to a musical Christmas story! A brother and sister, Andrew and Lisa, will take you through the holiday season using easy pre-reading Christmas songs. Share the Christmas spirit with Andrew and Lisa as they select their tree, go on a sleigh ride, and sing their favorite Yuletide songs.

Beautiful illustrations are provided throughout this pre-reading Christmas story. An added feature is that each large illustration contains hidden music symbols (♩ , ♩ , ♩. , o , 𝄞 , 𝄢). The student is challenged to find and circle these through questions at the bottom of the page.

Pre-Reading Christmas, A First Book for Piano, is an excellent preparation for on-the-staff reading. The student plays in Middle C Position and C Position. No eighth notes or dotted rhythms are used. The last three Christmas songs introduce the staff in combination with some letter names.

This provides a smooth transition into conventional note reading. Teacher duets offer ensemble opportunity as well as rhythmic vitality.

Pre-Reading Christmas, A First Book for Piano, is part of the *Pre-Reading Music Stories* Series written and arranged by Nancy and Randall Faber. "Pre-reading" designates off-the-staff reading through letter names and directional reading. Pre-reading graduates may move directly into the *PreTime®* to *BigTime®* *Piano Supplementary Library*. A complete listing is shown on the back of this book.

Helpful Hints:

1. Time signatures are not given at the pre-reading level. If the teacher desires, the student may write them in at the beginning of each piece.

2. This pre-reading musical Christmas story is ideal for a holiday recital. The selections may be divided among the pre-reading performers and narrated by the students themselves. The last piece, "Merry Christmas to You," might be sung by students and audience. Older brothers and sisters can be encouraged to play the duets.

3. Another festive idea for students is a musical Christmas tape. A cassette recording can be a treasured gift for relatives while giving a sense of accomplishment to the student.

ISBN 978-1-61677-050-1

Table of Contents

Big soft snowflakes were falling as Andrew and Lisa walked home from school.

"I can't wait until December 25th!" Andrew said happily. "Lisa, how many more days until Christmas?"

"I can tell you how many," his sister exclaimed.

Then Lisa began singing this song for her younger brother.

DISCOVERY! Can you find and circle all the half-notes (𝅗𝅥 or 𝅗) in this picture? There are six.

Counting the Days

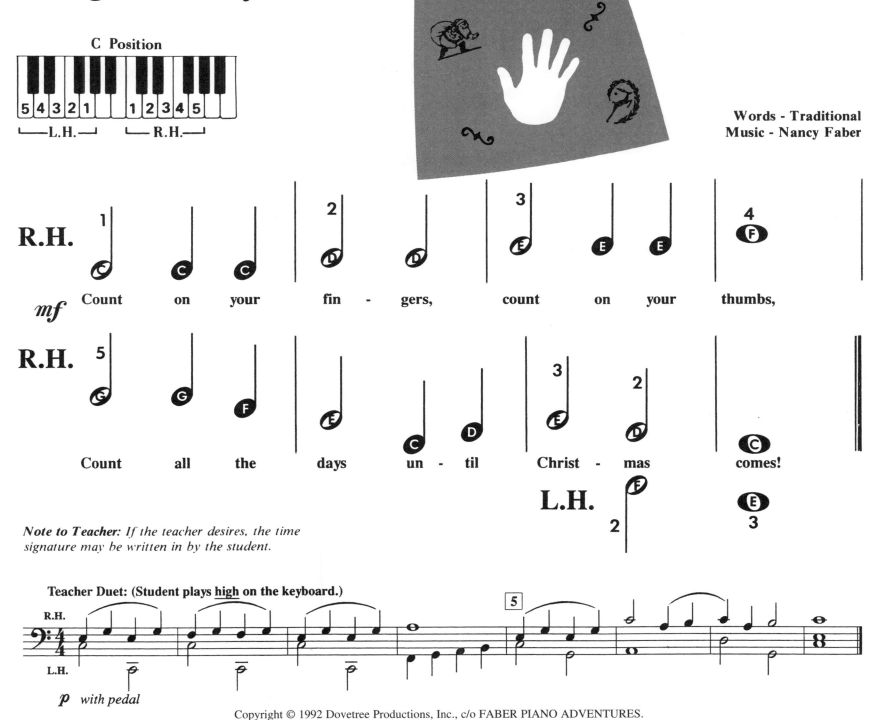

Words - Traditional
Music - Nancy Faber

Note to Teacher: If the teacher desires, the time signature may be written in by the student.

050

$\mathcal{A}$ndrew and Lisa go to choir practice every Wednesday night. This week they sang Christmas songs and ate cookies with hot chocolate after the rehearsal.

The next three songs are some of their favorites.

DISCOVERY! Can you find and circle all the dotted half-notes (𝅗𝅥. or ♩.) in this picture? There are eight.

Deck the Halls

Teacher Duet: (Student plays <u>high</u> on the keyboard.)

050

7

Good King Wenceslas

Traditional

Good King Wen - ces - las looked out on the feast of Ste - phen,
When the snow lay 'round a - bout, deep and crisp and e - ven.

f - p on repeat

Teacher Duet: (Student plays high on the keyboard.)

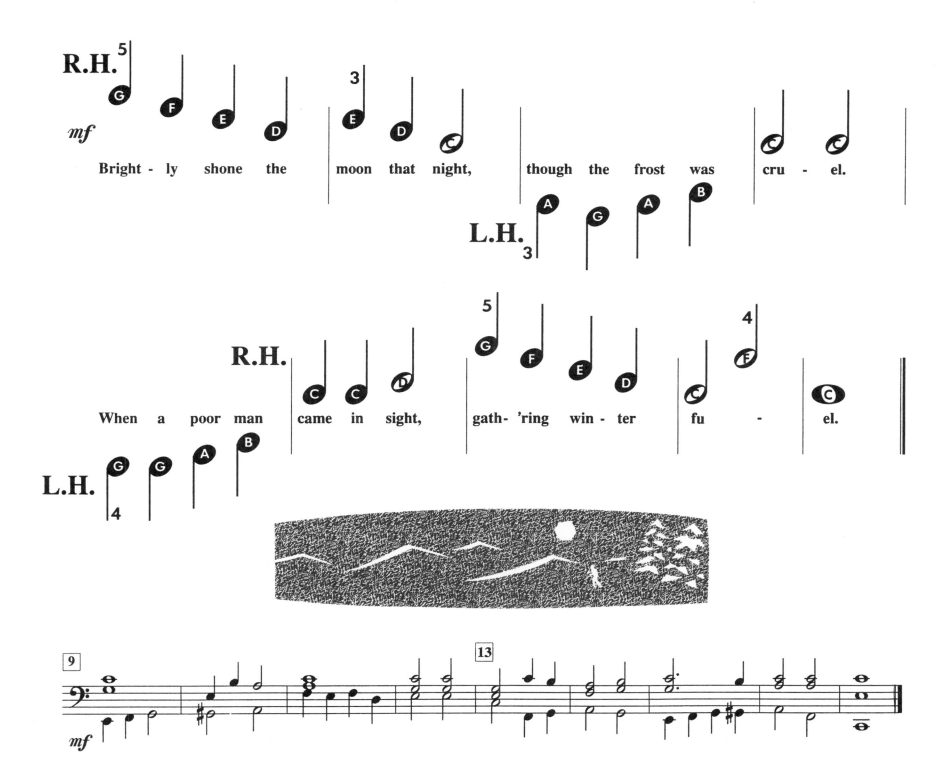

Away in a Manger

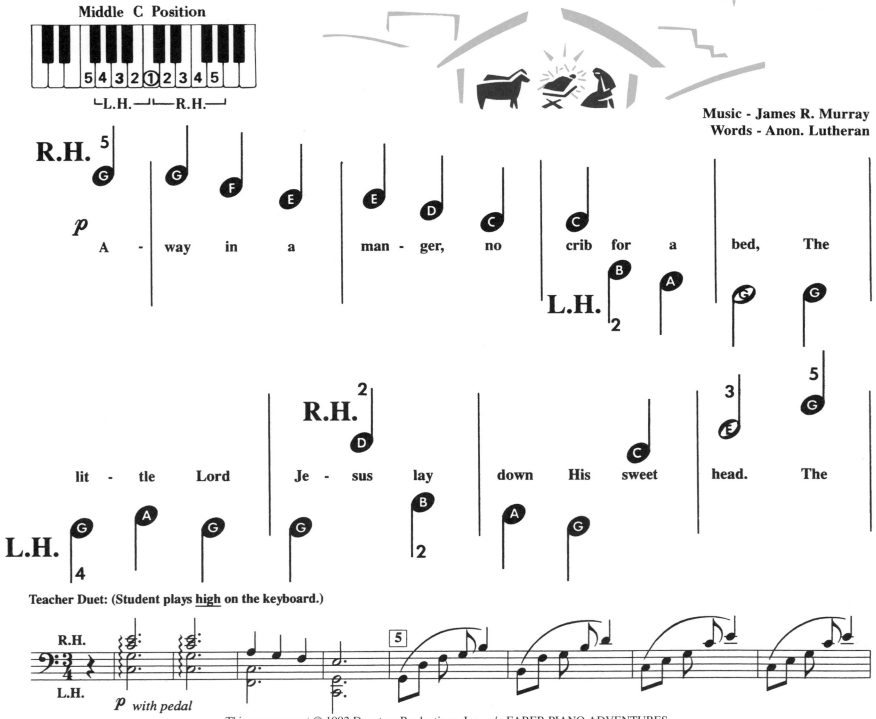

On Saturday night they went with their parents for a sleighride in the countryside.

All the houses looked magical in the moonlight and the sleighbells on the big horses jingled as they trotted along.

Can you guess what song they sang in the sleigh? _____

_____

DISCOVERY! Can you find and circle all the quarter notes (♩ or ♩) in this picture? There are twenty.

Jingle Bells

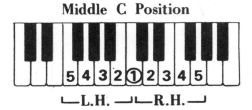

Middle C Position

Words and Music by
J. Pierpont

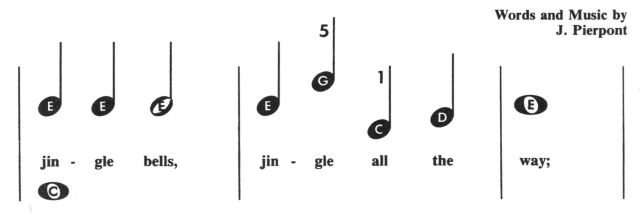

mf

R.H.

Jin - gle bells, jin - gle bells, jin - gle all the way;

L.H.

R.H.

Oh, what fun it is to ride in a one - horse o - pen sleigh!——

Teacher Duet: (Student plays <u>high</u> on the keyboard.)

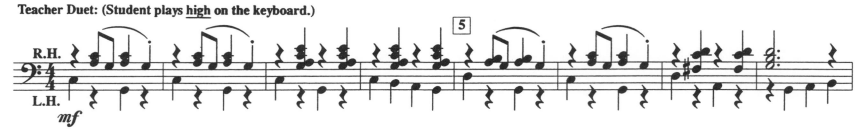

R.H.

L.H.

mf

FFI

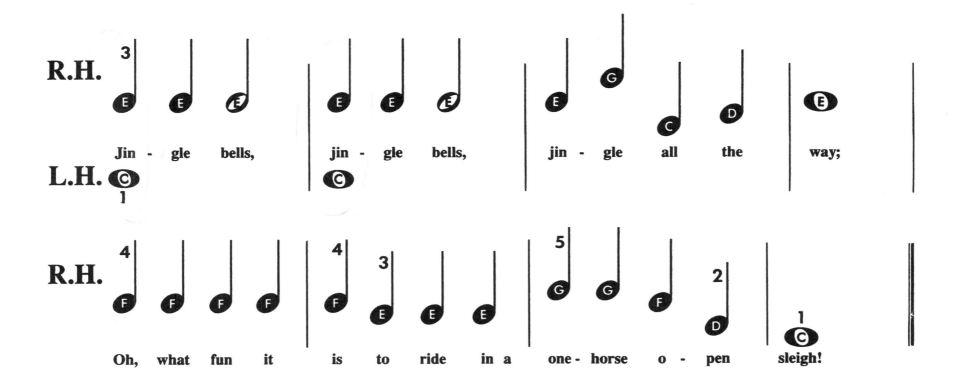

$\mathcal{S}$unday afternoon Lisa and **Andrew** went with their parents to a Christmas tree farm. There were rows of green fir trees, spruces, and northern pines.

As the family began hunting for the perfect Christmas tree, they sang this song:

DISCOVERY! Can you find and circle all the whole notes ($\mathbf{O}$) in this picture? **There are eight.**

The Tree Hunt

Words and Music by
Nancy Faber

R.H. f We're on a tree hunt; We're on a tree hunt.

R.H. Let's find the per - fect Christ - mas tree.

Teacher Duet: (Student plays high on the keyboard.)

That night they decorated their Christmas tree with many-colored lights, popcorn, and tinsel. They put an angel at the very top!

The Perfect Christmas Tree

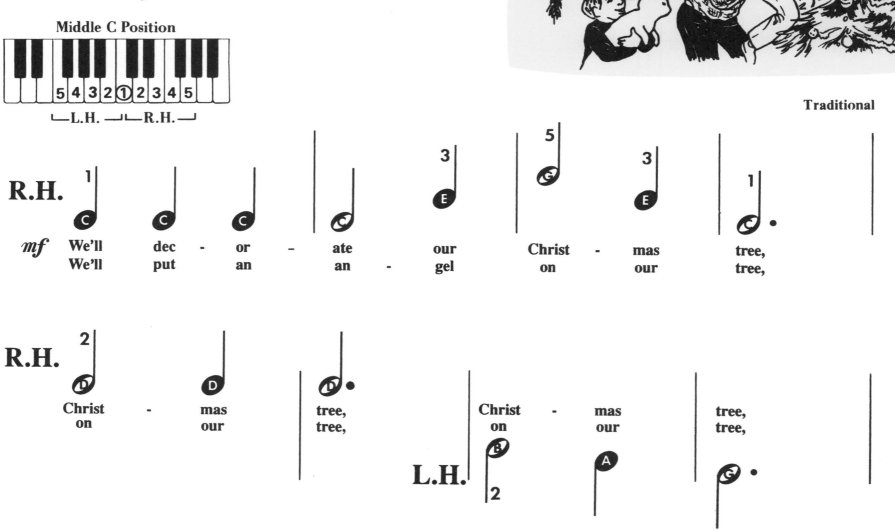

Traditional

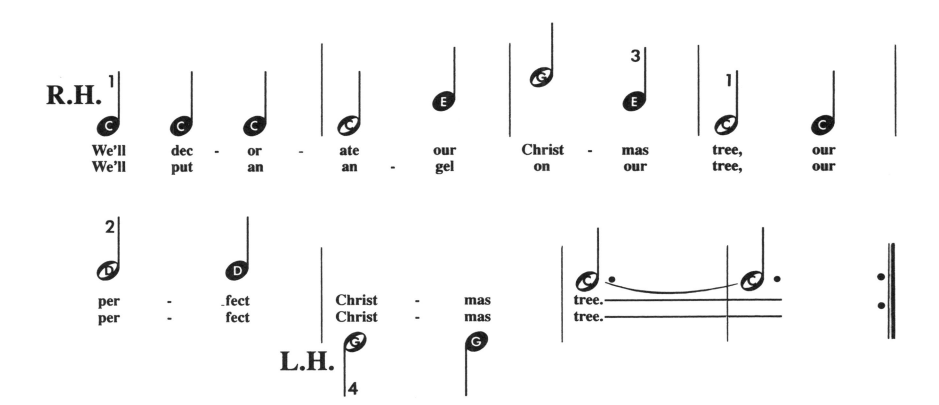

We'll dec - or - ate our Christ - mas tree, our
We'll put an an - gel on our tree, our

per - fect Christ - mas tree.
per - fect Christ - mas tree.

Teacher Duet: (Student plays <u>high</u> on the keyboard.)

mp with pedal

Then Lisa and Andrew each made out a Christmas list for Santa Claus that looked like this:

Jolly Old Saint Nicholas

Middle C Position

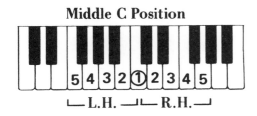

Happily

Traditional

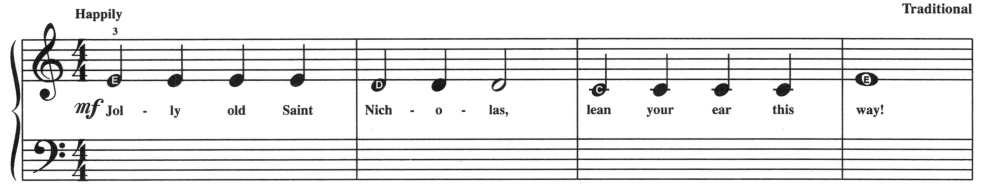

mf Jol - ly old Saint Nich - o - las, lean your ear this way!

FF1

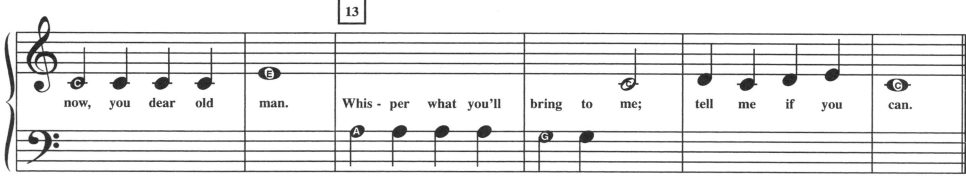

Teacher Duet: (Student plays **1** octave higher.)

On Christmas Eve, Lisa and Andrew sang in the children's choir for a special church service. The boys sang loudly from the front of the church. The girls echoed softly from the top of the balcony.

DISCOVERY! Can you find each of the following hidden in this picture?

Ring the Bells!

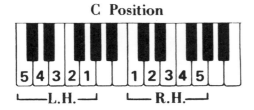

C Position

5 4 3 2 1   1 2 3 4 5
└── L.H. ──┘ └── R.H. ──┘

Words - Traditional
Music - Nancy Faber

Joyfully

Ring the bells! Ring the bells! This is Christ - mas Day!

Be sure to play the *f* and *p* signs.

Ring the bells! Ring the bells! This is Christ - mas Day!

Teacher Duet: (Student plays as written.)

f - *p* on repeat

When Christmas morning finally came, Andrew woke Lisa up very early. They raced into their parents room singing...

Merry Christmas to You

Middle C Position

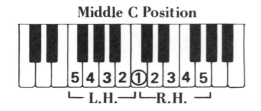

5 4 3 2 1 2 3 4 5
└ L.H. ┘└ R.H. ┘

Traditional

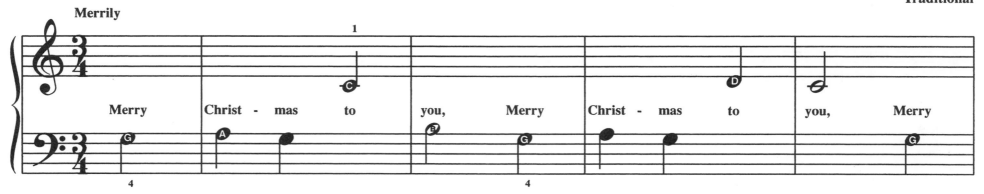

Merrily

Merry Christ - mas to you, Merry Christ - mas to you, Merry

Christ - mas every - bod - y, Merry Christ - mas to you!

The family opened their presents and had a big Christmas meal. At the end of the day, Andrew yawned and said sleepily, "I can't wait until next Christmas. Lisa, how many more days?"

FF